Picturing Baseball:
A Personal View in 100 Photographs

Compiled and Introduced by Richard R. Schieffelin

Privately Published to Accompany Home Display

This catalogue is privately published in a limited edition
to accompany the home display of 100 baseball photographs
at 11104 Sewickley Place, Fairfax, Virginia, 22030.
All photos were selected and arranged by Richard R. Schieffelin;
the framing was done by the Art and Framing Center of Stafford, Virginia;
Broadway Gallery of Alexandria, Virginia installed the display on August 16, 2023;
and the contextual photos on pages 4, 18, and 22 were taken by Sean Kelley Photography.

RRS, December 15, 2023

Front cover photo of Babe Ruth **(25A)** by Nickolas Murray
Back cover photo of Mariano Rivera **(12A)** by Anthony J. Causi

Copyright © 2023 Richard R. Schieffelin
All rights reserved.
ISBN: 9798854754095

Dedicated to the memory of my Uncle,

John A. Hunt,

who loved baseball and the New York Yankees

Contents

Introduction	iii
Part 1 Reading the Walls	**1**
Baseball from 1903 to the Mid-1970s	3
The New York Yankees from the 1920s to 2007	9
Babe Ruth	17
Baseball in America	21
Part 2 Reference Indexes	**25**
Directory by Column and Row	25
Alphabetical List of Subjects	31
Part 3 Photo Gallery	**33**

Illustrations

Family Room with photographs	iii
Dizzy Dean **(8B)**	iv
Carl Hubbell **(9B)**	iv
Hank Greenberg **(9C)**	iv
Ted Williams **(9D)**	iv
Joe McCarthy, Casey Stengel, and Bill Terry **(15C)**	iv
Bill Dickey, Lefty Gomez, and Lou Gehrig **(19B)**	iv
Tris Speaker **(4B)**	iv
Willie Mays **(10D)**	iv
Joe Gordon **(16C)**	iv
Phil Rizzuto **(16D)**	iv
Joe DiMaggio in action **(17C, 18C, 19C, 20C)**	v
Wall 1: Baseball from 1903 to the Mid-1970s	4
Greatest Pitchers of the Dead Ball Era	5
Bill Terry **(8A)** of the New York Giants	7
Hank Aaron **(11C)** of the Milwaukee Braves	8
Wall 2: The New York Yankees from the 1920s to 2007	10
Miller Huggins **(21A)** (1918-1929	11
Joe McCarthy **(20A)** (1931-1945)	11
Casey Stengel (1949-1960)	11

Joe Torre **(14A)** (1996-2007) 11
Wall 3: Babe Ruth 18
Wall 4: Baseball in America. 22
Mariano Rivera **(12A)** of the Yankees, was the last player to wear No. 42 136

Introduction

The home display of baseball photographs, magazine covers, and prints, shown below and described in this catalogue, evolved over time. It went from a few photos reclaimed from my work office to decorate the family room to a comprehensive, though highly personal, narrative of baseball in the 20th century—from 1903, when Major League Baseball first established itself as the combined American and National Leagues, through the mid-1970s. The size of the room and open wall space severely constrained the scope of the story and limited my selections to 100 photographs; and while most all of the players included would be on everyone's Top 100 List, this was not an exercise to pick my 100 best players. The individual players' stories and the overall development of baseball and its place in our modern culture were the controlling principles.

Part 1, "Reading the Walls," explains the organization of the four walls and briefly reviews the significance of the subjects in the photos. It is not a detailed history of the subjects. Wall 1—Baseball from 1903 to the Mid-1970s—addresses both American and National League players and teams. Wall 2—The New York Yankees from the 1920s to 2007—traces the Yankees from the beginning of their winning ways in the 1920s into the 21st century. Wall 3 spotlights Babe Ruth, the greatest baseball player, who is fairly credited with saving the game from the fallout over the 1919 Black Sox Scandal and introducing an exciting new style of play based on offense and the home run. Wall 4—Baseball in America—illustrates baseball in American culture in photos, magazine covers, and prints from the late 19th and 20th centuries.

Family Room with photographs.

Some of the images are signed collectables, but that was not a significant consideration. The players, teams, and historic moments that best represented the display themes were the leading selection criteria, followed by how to most tellingly illustrate them and create visual variety in perspective and layout as a total group. With few exceptions, the photos are black and white, and the images are mostly eight by ten inches to maximize the number that could be included.

Overwhelmingly the photos are of individual players and the specific photos were selected to depict their characteristic countenances. Some of the best photos present their stern game faces. The set of rookie photos of Dizzy Dean **(8B)**, Carl Hubbell **(9B)**, Hank Greenberg **(9C)**, and Ted Williams **(9D)**, all taken by Charles M. Conlon in the 1930s, are particularly revealing.

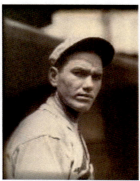

Dizzy Dean (8B)   **Carl Hubbell (9B)**

Hank Greenberg (9C)   **Ted Williams (9D)**

Pleasure was also part of the game as seen in the joyful expressions of the baseball-wise managers Joe McCarthy, Casey Stengel, and Bill Terry **(15C)** in the 1950s; and the Yankee greats Bill Dickey, Lefty Gomez, and Lou Gehrig **(19B)** in their prime in the early 1930s.

L to R: Joe McCarthy, Casey Stengel, and Bill Terry (15C)

L to R: Bill Dickey, Lefty Gomez, and Lou Gehrig (19B)

Action photos were sometimes used to most effectively portray the essence of a ballplayer. For example: Tris Speaker **(4B)** racing in on a fly ball; Willie Mays **(10D)** aggressively sliding home; Joe Gordon **(16C)** making the pivot at second base; and Phil Rizzuto **(16D)** dropping a bunt.

Tris Speaker (4B)   **Willie Mays (10D)**

Joe Gordon (16C)   **Phil Rizzuto (16D)**

Introduction

An action sequence best suited Joe DiMaggio (**17C**), who was sheer elegance on the ballfield. In the photos below, he gracefully swings (**18C**), rounds first (**19C**), and slides home (**20C**).

Joe DiMaggio in action.

The all-important theme of team work is highlighted by five ball clubs: 1906 Chicago Cubs (**2A**); 1929 Philadelphia Athletics (**6A**); and the New York Yankees of 1927 (**22A**), 1939 (**18A**), and 1961 (**13B**). They won across multiple seasons and were arguably the best teams ever fielded.

A number of the photos capture historic moments, such as: the opening of Yankee Stadium (**26A**) in 1923; Babe Ruth (**23C**) hitting his 60th home run and Roger Maris (**12C**) his 61st, President Franklin D. Roosevelt (**26B**) throwing out the ceremonial first pitch of the 1938 season; and Ruth's (**25C**) sad farewell at Yankee Stadium in 1948.

For the most reliable biographical summaries and up-to-date statistics of the teams and players, see the websites maintained by the Society for American Baseball Research (SABR) and Baseball Reference. They are available at https://sabr.org/ and https://www.baseball-reference.com/. SABR also maintains a rich digital archive of more than 80,000 photographs, which can be accessed at https://sabr.org/rucker-archive. The Baseball Hall of Fame has placed over 300,000 photos from their vast collection online at photoarchives@baseballhall.org.

The columns on the walls are consecutively numbered **1-28**, moving continuously L to R, clockwise, around the room. The rows are labeled **A-E**, from top to bottom. See the four contextual photos in Part 1, "Reading the Walls," for orientation. The numbers at the top of the photos indicate the **Columns 1-28**. Column and row citations to the photographs have been bolded throughout for easy reference.

The Reference Indexes in Part 2 present a Directory by Column and Row and an Alphabetical List of Subjects to identify and locate the photographs on the walls.

Each of the 100 photographs is reproduced in the Photo Gallery in Part 3. They are ordered by the sequential column and row positions they hold on the walls, **1A-28B**.

Several people were especially helpful in planning and executing this project. At the Baseball Hall of Fame in Cooperstown, New York, Library Director Cassidy Lent supported two important early research trips to survey the photographs in their files; and John Horne, Coordinator of Rights and Reproduction, promptly responded to my copy requests.

My friends, Jim W. Whalen and Steve Klein, kindly gave the final draft of the introductory essay a close reading and improved the text and saved me from several errors in fact.

As in all my projects, Laura Mathews has been a valued partner and challenged me to make this a better product by her professional preparation of the manuscript for publication.

And finally, I want to thank my wife, Josie, for graciously giving over so much wall space in the most common area of the house, and tolerating the long windup to deliver the display.

Richard R. Schieffelin
Fairfax, VA
December 15, 2023

Part 1

Reading the Walls

1. Baseball from 1903 to the Mid-1970s
2. The New York Yankees from the 1920s to 2007
3. Babe Ruth
4. Baseball in America

Wall 1
Baseball from 1903 to the Mid-1970s

Wall 1: Baseball from 1903 to the Mid-1970s *(Photo by Sean Kelley Photography)*.

Wall 1: Baseball from 1903 to the Mid-1970s *(Columns 1-11)*. See the photo opposite for the setup of Wall 1. The centerpiece is the oversized portrait of Christy Mathewson **(6C)** by Charles M. Conlon, surrounded by photos of Charles "Chief" Bender **(5C)**, Walter "The Big Train" Johnson **(5D)**, Grover Cleveland Alexander **(7C)**, and Mordecai "Three Finger" Brown **(7D)**. See the photo below.

Greatest Pitchers of the Dead Ball Era.

These five were the greatest pitchers of the first years of the 20th century, when pitchers ruled over the hitters. It was the Dead Ball Era, which ran from approximately 1903 to 1920. Frank "Home Run" Baker **(4A)**, the leading power hitter of the period, led the American League in home runs four consecutive years, from 1911 to 1914, and never hit more than 12 in a season. The photos directly above the five pitchers, and to the left **(Columns 1-7)**, cover the years 1903 to 1929; while the photos to the right **(Columns 8-11)** are from the 1930s to the mid-1970s.

1903 through the 1920s *(Columns 1 through 7)*. These columns begin in the upper left corner with the 1903 photo of Christy Mathewson, John McGraw, and "Iron Man" Joe McGinnity **(1A)**, all of the New York Giants, and extend through Column 7 and the photo of "Three Fingered" Brown **(7D)**.

The Chicago Cubs **(2A)** won an incredible 116 games in 1906 and five National League pennants between 1906 and 1918 (1906, 1907, 1908, 1910, and 1918). Their 1906 season was never surpassed in the 154-game era. In the World Series of 1906, they were matched up against their cross-town rivals, the Chicago White Sox. In one of the biggest upsets in sports history, the Cubs lost in six games. They went on to win back-to-back World Series in 1907 and 1908, the first team to appear in three consecutive World Series, and the first to win twice. They would not win their third World Series until over 100 years in 2016.

Edward M. "Ted" Lewis **(3A)** known as "Parson" and "The Pitching Professor" pitched for the Boston Braves from 1896 to 1900, and then the Boston Red Sox in 1901. He compiled an overall 93-63 record, and in 1897 and 1898 went 20-12 and 25-8. When he left baseball, the college-educated Lewis taught rhetoric and literature before becoming a college administrator. He became president of the University of New Hampshire in 1927 and served until his death in 1936. Though a fine pitcher, Lewis is on the wall because of a personal association. He was the great uncle of my late close friend and serious student of early baseball, Hobie L. Morris.

Popularized by extensive newspaper and magazine coverage at the turn of the 20th century, baseball offered the public, which was increasingly concentrated in the cities, both mass entertainment and new athletic heroes. Attendance at Major League games went over three million in 1901, and by 1907 more than seven million were going to games each year. Honus Wagner **(1B, 2B, and 3B)** and Napoleon "Nap" Lajoie **(2C)** were the earliest superstars. Wagner was the first nationally popular athlete of the 20th century. He played shortstop for the Pittsburgh Pirates from 1897 to 1917 and won eight batting titles. Lajoie played second base from 1896 to 1916, first for the Philadelphia Athletics and then Cleveland. He led the American League in batting five times; and in 1901 he set the modern era record with a .426 batting average. Lajoie's yearly battles with Ty Cobb **(1D)** for the batting title were headline news; and their competition in 1910, in the words of baseball historian Rick Huhn, was a "national obsession."

Eddie Collins **(1C)** was active between 1906 and 1930 and starred for Connie Mack's early champion Philadelphia Athletics (1906-1914) and then the Chicago White Sox. Mack ranked him "the greatest second baseman." John McGraw, after his Giants lost to Mack's Athletics in the 1913 World Series, said: "I want to go on record as saying that Collins is the greatest ballplayer in the world."

An innocent looking Ty Cobb is shown in **(1D)**. His combative temperament and willful determination to be the best—not yet visible in this 1905 rookie photo—would make him the dominant performer in baseball before 1920. He won 11 batting titles and holds the all-time record with a .367 lifetime batting average.

"Shoeless" Joe Jackson **(2D)**, illiterate and unworldly, batted .408 in his first full Major League season (1911) with the Cleveland Naps. "Shoeless" Joe's swing was much admired by Babe Ruth, and Ty Cobb called him "the finest natural hitter in the history of the game." Jackson moved to the Chicago White Sox in 1915, where he was tragically caught up in the 1919 Black Sox Scandal. He was banned from baseball after the 1920 season and in subsequent years became a sympathetic cult figure. Groups continue to regularly petition baseball to reinstate Joe Jackson and the Hall of Fame to induct him. His .356 lifetime batting average ranks third, behind Ty Cobb and Rogers Hornsby.

"Gorgeous" George Sisler **(3C)** is considered by many the most talented first baseman to ever play. His career (1916-1930) straddled the Dead Ball and Live Ball Eras, and he was the first athlete featured on the cover of *Time Magazine* (1925). The selection registered his celebrity and reflected the country's enthusiasm for sports—particularly baseball—that had come to occupy American culture in the 1920s. His lifetime batting average was .340, and he topped .400 twice (.407 in 1920 and .420 in 1922). Sisler received the inaugural American League Trophy as the league's MVP for his historic performance in 1922, when he led the typically abysmal St. Louis Browns to what was far and away their best season in franchise history.

Tris Speaker **(4B)** was a marvel, and perhaps the best all-around player in baseball history. He played from 1909 through 1927, first for the Boston Red Sox and then the Cleveland Indians. An absolute wizard in center field, he had a great sense for the flight of the baseball and incredible closing speed. Speaker also had a strong and strikingly accurate throwing arm—his 449 outfield assists is still the record. And he was one of the best hitters to ever play, too. The superbly athletic Speaker retired with 3,514 hits and a .345 lifetime batting average, both fifth on the all-time list.

Rogers Hornsby **(4C)** is almost universally regarded as the greatest right-handed hitter of all time. He was the National League's foremost star in the 1920s—their answer to Babe Ruth. Like the Babe and George Sisler, Hornsby's time in the majors bridged the Dead Ball and Live Ball Eras. His first full year in the Major Leagues was 1916 and his principal playing days were over by 1930. He hit better than .400 three times, won seven batting titles, and retired with a .358 lifetime batting average. Hornsby was notorious for his brusque manner, intensity of play, and single-minded devotion to winning.

Photo **(3D)** was taken at the opening of the Baseball Hall of Fame in Cooperstown, New York in 1939. It neatly summarizes the finest players of the game from 1903 through the 1920s: Eddie Collins, Babe Ruth, Connie Mack, Cy Young, Honus Wagner, Grover Cleveland Alexander, Tris Speaker, Nap Lajoie, George Sisler, and Walter Johnson. Ty Cobb missed the photo. A physical Hall of Fame—complete with artifacts, historical exhibits, and player relics—for an adoring public to visit, signified the cherished place baseball and its earliest heroes had achieved in society through the first decades of the twentieth century.

The 1929 Philadelphia Athletics **(6A)** squad was another exceptional team. They were led by Connie Mack **(5A)**, the "dean of the American League managers." This was Mack's second dynasty. The first won four pennants (1910, 1911, 1913, and 1914) and three World Series (1910, 1911, and 1913) between 1910 and 1914. This second dynasty unseated the Murderers' Row Yankees of the 1920s as baseball's premier team, and won American League pennants in 1929, 1930, and 1931, and the World Series in 1929 and 1930. Their standout players were pitcher Lefty Grove **(7A)**, whose won-loss record during the 1929-1931 seasons was an astounding 84-15, and sluggers Jimmie Foxx **(5B and 7B)**, Mickey Cochrane, and Al Simmons (both shown in **6B** with Foxx). The Depression forced Mack to sell off his star players to preserve the franchise.

Early 1930s through the Mid-1970s *(Columns 8-11).* Bill Terry **(8A)** marks the transition from the earlier decades. He came into the National League toward the end of the 1920s, and through the 1930s he was the best first baseman in the league and one of the biggest names in the game. He played first base with easy grace and hit .401 in 1930, the last National Leaguer to hit over .400. That year the entire National League batted .303. Ten years out from the end of the Dead Ball Era, offense decidedly prevailed over pitching.

Bill Terry of the New York Giants (8A).

In 1932, Terry succeeded the legendary John McGraw as manager of the New York Giants; and, with the additions of Mel Ott **(9A)** and Carl Hubbell **(9B)**, the Giants were briefly competitive again. They won pennants in 1933, 1936, and 1937, and the World Series in 1933. Ott led the National League in home runs six times and was the first National Leaguer to hit 500 home runs. When he retired in 1946, his 511 home runs were 200 more than the next highest National Leaguer.

Hubbell **(9B)**, known for his masterful screwball, was the foremost left-handed pitcher in the National League in the 1930s. He won the MVP award in 1933 and again in 1936, and set the incredible record of 24 consecutive wins across the 1936 and 1937 seasons. His most dramatic moment came in the 1934 All-Star Game **(8C)** when he struck out the five best American League hitters in succession: Babe Ruth, Lou Gehrig, Jimmie Foxx, Al Simmons, and Joe Cronin.

Other stars emerged in the 1930s, too. The brash Dizzy Dean **(8B)** debuted with the St. Louis Cardinals in 1930. In 1934 he had a 30-7 record—the last National League pitcher to win 30 games—and led the "Gas House Gang" to the pennant and victory over the Detroit Tigers in the World Series. After his playing days, Dean became a hugely popular radio and television personality delighting baseball audiences with entertaining country expressions and untamed grammar. He partnered with Pee Wee Reese for the CBS and NBC Game of the Week from the 1940s through 1965, which brought baseball into the homes of millions of fans.

Hank Greenberg **(9C)** is one of the most significant Jewish athletes in American history. He faced ugly Jew-baiting and relentless anti-Semitism throughout his career from fans and players alike—yet he remained focused on the game, setting a dignified example for future players like Jackie Robinson. Greenberg played first base for the Detroit Tigers from 1933 to 1941, and then again in 1945 and 1946, after his distinguished military service in World War II. One of the most feared power hitters in the history of the game, he made a serious run at Babe Ruth's home run record in 1938, but ended short with 58. With Greenberg in the lineup, the Tigers won pennants in 1934, 1935, 1940, and 1945. Their 1934 pennant was their first since 1909. In 1935 and 1945, they won the World Series.

Stan Musial **(8D)** and Ted Williams **(9D)** made it to the Major Leagues at the end of the decade. Williams' rookie year was 1939. He was the last American Leaguer to hit over .400 (.406 in 1941). Musial came into the National League in 1941. They were the best hitters of their generation. Williams played through the 1960 season and Musial 1963.

Williams won six batting titles, four home run crowns, the Triple Crown twice, and two MVP awards. The "Splendid Splinter" hit 521 home runs and had a lifetime batting average of .344. His astonishing career OBP of .482 remains the Major League record.

Musial won three MVP awards and seven batting titles. His 3,630 hits is fourth on the all-time list and his 725 doubles is second only to Tris Speaker's 793. "Stan the Man" had a lifetime batting average of .331, and he hit with power, too, ending his career with 475 homers.

Satchel Paige (10A) and Josh Gibson (11A) were the most notable players of Negro League baseball from the 1920s to the mid-1940s. Of the two, only Paige, when well beyond his prime, was given the token opportunity to play in the Major Leagues. The belated integration of Black athletes into Major League baseball finally happened in 1947 when Branch Rickey (11B), of the Brooklyn Dodgers, signed Jackie Robinson to a Major League contract. Robinson, always an exciting base runner, is shown stealing home (10B), in the first game of the 1955 World Series against the New York Yankees. Yogi Berra is the catcher. The safe call is still hotly disputed.

With so many Major League players in service during World War II, baseball executives organized the All-American Girls Professional Baseball League (AAGPBL) in 1943 to maintain interest in the game. The AAGPBL ran from 1943 to 1954 and Faye Dancer (10C) was one of its brightest stars. She was nicknamed "All the Way Faye" for her on—and off—the field enthusiasm. Dancer was the model for the Madonna character, "All the Way Mae", in the 1992 hit movie, *A League of Their Own*. Dancer could hit for power, run, throw, and catch. She played from 1944 to 1950, and in 2002 was the second woman inducted into the National Women's Baseball Hall of Fame. Her fiancé—the love of her life—was killed in World War II. She never married. The inscribed photo (10C) to Josie, my wife, was a personal gift from Dancer, who was a family friend.

Wall 1 ends with two superstars of the second half of the 20th century—Willie Mays (10D) and Hank Aaron (11C). Both played in the Negro American League before coming to the Majors, but unlike other early MLB Black players—such as Robinson, Larry Doby, Roy Campenella, Minnie Minoso, and Monte Irvin—neither lost Major League playing time because of the color barrier. Both were excellent outfielders and demonstrated remarkable power and consistency at the plate, and speed on the bases. In other words, both Mays and Aaron were all-around players. The dynamic Mays played from 1951 through 1973, and Aaron from 1954 through 1976.

Mays was the National League Rookie of the Year in 1951. He went on to bat a career .302 with 660 home runs and win four home run crowns, a batting title, two MVP awards, and 12 Gold gloves. No player was ever more exciting to watch.

Aaron's sustained excellence broke all power records (755 HRs and 2,297 RBIs) and he accumulated 3,771 hits, for a .305 career average. Aaron was the National League MVP in 1957, and won two batting titles, four home run crowns, and three Gold Gloves.

Hank Aaron of the Milwaukee Braves (11C).

Wall 2
The New York Yankees
from
the 1920s to 2007

Wall 2: The New York Yankees from the 1920s to 2007.

Wall 2: The New York Yankees from the 1920s to 2007 *(Columns 12-22).* See the photo on the opposite page for the layout of Wall 2. The chronology moves backward in time, L to R, from the large photograph of No. 42, Mariano Rivera **(12A),** entering the game, to the steely-eyed manager, Miller Huggins, in street clothes **(21A),** and the 1927 Yankees **(22A).**

The photos are arranged into subsections that correspond to the four fabulous eras in New York Yankee history: 1920s, mid-1930s through the 1940s, the 1950s to 1964, and 1996 to 2007. The 30 year down period from 1965 to 1995 is also covered. To date, the Yankees have won 40 American League pennants and 27 World Championships, making them the most successful sports franchise in history. The team in each of these eras was led by one of the great field managers shown below.

Miller Huggins (21A)
(1918-1929)

Joe McCarthy (20A)
(1931-1945)

Casey Stengel
(1949-1960)

Joe Torre (14A)
(1996-2007)

The discussion sections below follow Wall 2 from right to left, in chronological order from the oldest coverage in the 1920s **(22A),** to the most recent in the 21st century **(12A).**

Miller Huggins Years, 1918-1929 *(Columns 22 and 21).* During the 1920s, the Yankees went from an unremarkable second-division team to a championship dynasty. They won American League pennants in 1921, 1922, 1923, 1926, 1927, and 1928; and the World Series in 1923, 1927, and 1928. The transformation can be attributed to three strategic changes. First, the purchase of the team in 1917 by Jacob Ruppert and Tillinghast "Til" Huston established a firm foundation of closely engaged—but not interfering—owners with deep pockets, committed to building an enduring winner. Second, hiring Miller Huggins **(21A)** in 1918 put a first class field manager in place with an uncanny ability to evaluate player talent. Third, the acquisition of Babe Ruth from the Boston Red Sox in 1920 revolutionized attendance and the team's offense. Collectively Ruppert, Huggins, and Ruth were the difference-makers. They enabled the Yankees to win in the near term and continuously refresh their roster with some of baseball's top performers and prospects.

The lineup for the first part of the 1920s—that won pennants in 1921, 1922, and 1923—featured veterans nearing the end of their productive years, complemented with up-and-coming players. The veterans included pitchers Bob Shawkey and Carl Mays; catcher Wally Schang; infielders Frank "Home Run" Baker **(4A),** Everett Scott, and Wally Pipp; and outfielders Bing Podie and Whitey Witt. The key new arrivals were outfielders Babe Ruth and Bob Meusel **(22C group photo)** in 1920; third baseman Joe Dugan in 1922; and pitchers Waite Hoyt **(21D)** in 1921 and Herb Pennock **(22D)** in 1923.

Called "Long Bob" because of his 6-foot 3-inch stature, Meusel **(21B)** had an outstanding throwing arm and usually batted fifth. In 1925, he became the second Yankee (after Ruth) to lead the American League in home runs (33) and RBIs (134). His 1,009 RBIs during the 1920s were the fourth most by any Major Leaguer. He played for the Yankees until 1929 and retired with a .309 lifetime average.

Hoyt **(21D)** became a member of the Yankees' starting rotation in 1921, and over the next eight years averaged 18 wins and 253 innings a year.

His two best years were 1927 and 1928, when he went 22-7 and 23-7. He excelled in the World Series and earned a reputation as "a money pitcher." In retirement, Hoyt broadcast Cincinnati Reds games for 24 years (1942-1966).

Herb Pennock's **(22D)** prime years with the Yankees were from 1923 through 1928. He consistently issued the fewest walks in the league and was near the top each year in winning percentage. Pennock, too, was terrific in the World Series—winning five games and losing none.

By 1926, most of the players from the 1921-1923 teams had been replaced by budding stars to bring together the great Yankee teams of 1926, 1927, and 1928. In 1925 Earle Combs joined Ruth and Meusel in the outfield **(22C group photo)**. The fleet Combs batted leadoff and played his entire career (1925-1934) with the Yankees, retiring with a .325 lifetime batting average. Ruth in right, Meusel in left, and Combs in center constituted an extraordinary outfield.

"Jumpin" Joe Dugan remained at third through the 1928 season, but by 1926 all the other infield positions had turned over **(21C group photo)**. Lou Gehrig **(22B1 and 22B2)** took over for Wally Pipp as the regular Yankee first baseman in 1925, and went on to play in 2,130 consecutive games. A model of consistency and power, he batted fourth behind Babe Ruth. Tony Lazzeri **(21E)** became the second baseman in 1926. The Yankees purchased his contract for the then incredible sum of $50,000 after his astonishing 1925 season in the Pacific Coast League (60 HRs, .355 average, and 222 RBIs). Lazzeri would be the first Italian star in the Major Leagues. He was paired up with another rookie—Mark Koenig—at shortstop.

The 1927 Yankees **(22A)**—the standard for all great teams—won 110 games and lost only 44 for a .714 winning percentage. They had a team batting average of .307 and a 3.20 ERA. Both led the league. The '27 Yankees finished 19 games ahead of a very good Philadelphia Athletics team and swept the Pittsburgh Pirates in four straight in the World Series. Babe Ruth hit 60 home runs **(23C)**, drove in 165, and batted .356; but that was not good enough for the MVP award. That honor went to Lou Gehrig, who hit 47 home runs, drove in 173, and batted .373. Six players on the 1927 team became members of the Hall of Fame: Ruth, Gehrig, Hoyt, Pennock, Combs, and Lazzeri, as well as manager Huggins and team executive Ed Barrow.

The Yankees repeated in 1928 and soundly beat the Cardinals four straight in the World Series, avenging their 1926 loss to St. Louis. Across the 1927 and 1928 World Series, the Yankees won eight-straight games. The Athletics **(6A)** finally triumphed in 1929 and displaced the Yankees as the best team in baseball.

Just days before the end of the 1929 season, Miller Huggins **(21A)** died suddenly. His teams had won six pennants and three World Series in the last nine years. As the Yankee manager, he had won 1,067 games and lost 719 for a .597 winning percentage. Looking back, Jacob Ruppert commented: "From the day Huggins took charge of the team, the Yankees were on the upgrade." In 1932, Huggins was honored with an on-field monument in center field at Yankee Stadium, which stood alone for more than a decade until monuments to Lou Gehrig (1941) and Babe Ruth (1949) were set alongside.

Joe McCarthy Years, 1931-1945, through the end of the 1940s *(Columns 20-15)*. Ruth, Gehrig, and the offense kept the Yankees competitive, but the pitching staff disintegrated. Bob Shawkey managed the team to a disappointing third-place finish in 1930, while Ruppert and Barrow explored their options. Eventually they hired Joe McCarthy **(20A)** as the new manager, and it was a brilliant choice. Like his predecessor, Miller Huggins **(21A)**, McCarthy had wonderful insight into the players and a special knack for judging their abilities.

In 1931, McCarthy's first year, the Yanks won 94 games and finished second to Mack's Athletics. In 1932 they won 107 games, the pennant, and beat the Chicago Cubs in the World Series. Under McCarthy (1931-1945), the Yankees would win eight pennants and seven World Series, including four World Series in a row (1936-1939). In his tenure as the Yankee skipper, McCarthy won 1,460 games against only 867 loses for a staggering .627 winning percentage. His career winning percentage, including his time managing the Chicago Cubs and Boston Red Sox, was .615—the highest among Major League managers.

It would be 1936 before the Yankees were solidly back on top. While they pieced their team back together, they finished second in 1933 to the Washington Senators, and second again in 1934 and 1935 to the Detroit Tigers. McCarthy had a strong core to build around: Gehrig and Lazzeri in the infield, Bill Dickey behind the plate, and the recently acquired pitchers Red Ruffing (20B) and Vernon "Lefty" Gomez (19A). Photo (19B) shows Dickey, Gomez, and Gehrig enjoying themselves in the early 1930s. The outfield was more problematic. The highest profile change was Ruth—his final Yankee season was 1934. Also in 1934, star center fielder Earle Combs crashed into the wall at Sportsman's Park in St. Louis and suffered career-ending injuries.

Bill Dickey (22E) had become the front line catcher in 1929 and his rookie year was a fair indicator of his future greatness—.324 average, 10 home runs, and 66 RBIs, while striking out only 16 times. Over his career, in 7,065 plate appearances, Dickey struck out only 289 times. He went on to catch 100 or more games for 13 consecutive seasons. An exceptional handler of pitchers and one of the best defensive catchers to ever play, Dickey's career fielding average was .988. He played 125 games in 1931 without a passed ball and was always a serious threat at the plate, too, for average and power. In 1936, he batted .362, still the high mark for a catcher, and his lifetime average was .313. He hit 202 home runs. Through the 1930s and into the 1940s, Dickey was an invaluable team leader.

Red Ruffing (20B) came to the Yankees from the Boston Red Sox in 1930 and quickly went from a struggling pitcher with a 39-96 record to one of the best pitchers in the American League. Ruffing had been originally recruited as an outfielder, but a mining accident cost him four toes on his left foot, so he could not run. Determined to still play Major League ball, he converted to pitching. He is credited with inventing and throwing one of the best sliders. Ruffing won 273 games and anchored the Yankee pitching staff into the 1940s. During the Yankees' record run of four consecutive pennants and World Series victories—1936 through 1939—he won 20 games or more each year, and was equally good in the World Series, winning seven games and losing only two.

Lefty Gomez (19A) joined the Yankees in 1931 and was an immediate sensation. Sometimes called "Goofy" for his colorful personality and sense of humor, the fire-balling lefthander won 20 or more games four times in the 1930s, and was 189 and 102 lifetime, for an incredible .649 winning percentage. Gomez's two best years were 1934 and 1937, when he won the pitching Triple Crown, leading the league in wins, ERA, and strikeouts. In 1934 he posted a 26-5 record with a 2.33 ERA. *Time Magazine* put him on their July 1934 cover (19A); and he started for the American League in the All-Star Game that year against Carl Hubbell of the Giants. Gomez was a perfect 6-0 in the World Series.

Spurgeon Ferdinand "Spud" Chandler (18B) joined Ruffing and Gomez in the starting rotation in 1937. Prone to arm trouble, Chandler pitched for the Yankees through 1947, but missed significant parts of several seasons. Manager McCarthy once commented that Ruffing, Gomez, and Chandler were the three smartest pitchers he saw in all his years in baseball. Chandler was on six World Series champion Yankee teams and was the American League's MVP in 1943. In his 10 years with the Yankees, Chandler won 109 games and lost only 43 for a .717 winning percentage, which remains the Major League record.

In 1932, Frank Crosetti (16A, 17B), another Bay Area Italian, took over at shortstop. The Yankee "holler guy" was a sure-handed fielder, but his weak hitting perpetually undermined his job security. Following his career at shortstop (1932-1940), Crosetti was a Yankee coach for decades. Red Rolfe (16B), a product of the new Yankee farm system, graduated from the Newark Bears in 1934 and became the everyday third baseman in 1935. He worked hard at his craft and was good with the glove—but even better with the bat. Rolfe's lifetime average was .289 and he rarely struck out. He was the top third baseman in the American League during his playing days (1934-1942), and the best who ever played for the Yankees. Gehrig and Lazzeri maintained their Hall of Fame level performances through the 1930s. The infield of Gehrig, Lazzeri, Rolfe, and Crosetti **(17B)** served the Yankees well through the 1930s.

George "Twinkle Toes" Selkirk **(17A group photo)** became the regular right fielder in 1935 and did a respectable job at the impossible task of replacing Babe Ruth. Over the next eight seasons, Selkirk hit above .300 five times, made the All-Star team in 1936 and 1939, and played on five world championship teams: 1936, 1937, 1938, 1939, and 1941.

The outfield and the overall team came together when Joe DiMaggio arrived in 1936 **(17C)**. The much heralded rookie from San Francisco was the third Bay Area Italian in the Yankee lineup, along with Lazzeri and Crosetti **(16A)**. "The Yankee Clipper's" graceful style and peerless performance **(18C, 19C, and 20C)** captivated fans and fellow players alike through 1951. He was an era-defining player—at bat for power and average, in the field running down balls and throwing, and on the bases.

During DiMaggio's 13 years with the Yankees, they won 10 pennants and nine World Series titles. Career highlights included: THE 56-game hitting streak in 1941, three MVP awards, two batting titles, and two home runs crowns. Joe D. stood straight and still in the batter's box with the bat held high, his feet were set wide apart in a closed stance, and when the ball was delivered, he took a quick, short, level swing. The approach generated great power and consistent contact. DiMaggio hit ferocious line drives to all fields and rarely struck out. In 1941, the year of his 56-game hitting streak, he struck out only 13 times in 622 at bats; and over his career, he struck out only 369 times in 7,672 at bats. His lifetime batting average was .325, and his 361 home runs placed him fifth on the all-time list at retirement, behind Babe Ruth (714), Jimmie Foxx (534), Mel Ott (511), and Lou Gehrig (493). Beyond the records and awards, DiMaggio transcended sport to become an iconic figure in popular culture.

With Gehrig, Lazzeri, Rolfe, and Crosetti **(17B group photo)** in the infield; DiMaggio and Selkirk in the outfield **(17A group photo)**; and Dickey catching Ruffing, Gomez, and Chandler, the team had no weaknesses. They easily won the American League pennant and World Series in 1936, 1937, 1938, and 1939. No team had ever won more than two World Series in a row. During this stretch, they finished on average 15 games ahead of the second-place American League teams, and across the four World Series they won 16 games and lost only three. The 1936 team featured six future Hall of Fame players (Gehrig, DiMaggio, Lazzeri, Dickey, Gomez, and Ruffing) and McCarthy, the manager. Many consider the last club in this run—1939 Yankees **(18A)**—the greatest team of all-time, to be seriously compared with the 1927 and 1961 championship Yankee teams.

In the 1940s, the Yankees won five more American League pennants (1941, 1942, 1943, 1947, and 1949) and another four World Series (1941, 1943, 1947, and 1949). Despite the championships, these were transition years. The great Gehrig stepped aside in 1939, the acrobatic Joe "Flash" Gordon **(16C)** replaced the aging Lazzeri at second base in 1938, and Phil "Scooter" Rizzuto **(16D)** displaced the popular veteran Crosetti at shortstop in 1941. Tommy "Old Reliable" Henrich **(15E1)** and Charlie Keller **(15E2)** came to the parent club through the Yankee farm system in 1938 and 1939, but did not get much playing time until 1941. With DiMaggio in center, and finally Henrich in right and Keller in left, the Yankees would have the best outfield in baseball for the next decade. Three additional players joined the team in 1946 and 1947 that would be key to the next dynasty in the 1950s: catcher Yogi Berra **(15D1)** in 1947, and pitchers Vic Raschi **(15D2)** in 1946 and Allie Reynolds **(16D)** in 1947. McCarthy left part way through the 1946 season after finishing third in 1944 and fourth in 1945. His record of eight pennants and seven World Series wins between 1931 and 1945 proved he and his teams were worthy successors to Miller Huggins and the great Yankee teams of the 1920s.

Casey Stengel Years, 1949-1960 *(Column 15).* The manager picked to follow McCarthy was Casey Stengel "The Old Professor" (Photo on p. 12 and in **15C group photo**). He was not an obvious choice, but proved another wise selection. A journeyman outfielder from 1912-1925, Stengel had tried his hand at managing after his playing days, but over 20 years enjoyed little success at it. The results were much different with the Yankees. Despite his clownish reputation, Stengel was an astute baseball man with innovative ideas that eventually became common practice across baseball—platooning players, five-man pitching rotation, and exploiting mismatches. In his 12 years at the helm (1949-1960), Stengel's teams won 10 pennants and seven World Series, including five World Series titles in a row (1949-1953). In total, his Yankee teams won 1,149 games while losing only 696 for a .623 win percentage.

Yogi Berra (**15D1**) had come to the parent team in 1947, and through hard work and the dedicated mentoring of Bill Dickey, he became the best catcher in baseball. No one was better at calling a game. Berra's career fielding percentage was .989, and he once handled 950 chances without an error over 148 games. And Yogi was a terrific hitter, particularly in high pressure situations. His hand-eye coordination was phenomenal, and he hit pitches in and out of the strike zone with equal ease. During his 17 years in the Majors, all with the Yankees, Berra struck out only 414 times in 8,364 plate appearances, hit 358 home runs, and batted .285. He won 10 World Series rings, the most of any player, and three MVP awards. When asked his secret to winning, Stengel replied, referring to Berra: "I never play a game without my man."

Elite starting pitching was fundamental to Stengel's success, and he began with two of the best in Vic Raschi (**15D2**) and Allie Reynolds (**16E**); and in 1950 he added a third—rookie Whitey Ford (**15B and 14D**). In his years with the Yankees (1946-1953), Raschi posted a stunning 120-50 record for a .706 winning percentage, which included a 92-40 record from 1949 to 1953, the years the Yankees won five World Series titles. Reynolds pitched for the Yankees from 1947 to 1954 and earned 131 wins against only 60 loses. His best year was 1951 when he pitched two no-hitters and was 20-8 with a 2.06 ERA. That year, Reynolds won the prestigious Hickok Belt as the top American professional athlete. He was 7-2 in his nine World Series starts. Called up toward the end of the 1950 season, Whitey Ford won his first nine starts and helped the Yankees win the pennant. He went on to win 236 games, the most in franchise history, and lose only 106, for an astounding .690 winning percentage.

In 1951, Joe DiMaggio retired and Mickey Mantle (**15A**)—the blonde "Commerce Comet"—burst onto the scene. Mantle would awe baseball fans with his speed and power through the mid-1960s. Despite crippling injuries throughout his career, Mantle won three MVP awards, the Triple Crown and Hickok Belt in 1956, and four home run crowns. His 536 home runs at retirement placed him third on the all-time list behind Willie Mays and Babe Ruth.

Elston Howard (**14D**) joined the Yankees in 1955 after playing in the Negro American League. He was Yogi Berra's successor behind the plate and the first Black player to wear a Yankee uniform. Howard was Stengel's ideal player type: he could hit, play multiple positions, and was smart. He was the American League MVP in 1963 and won Gold Gloves in 1963 and 1964. Howard's .993 career fielding percentage as a catcher stood as the Major League record from his retirement in 1967 to 1973.

Final Years of the Great Dynasty, 1961-1964 *(Photos 12C, 13C, and 14C).* Stengel retired after the 1960 World Series, and under Ralph Houk (1961-1963) and then Yogi Berra (1964) the Yankee's kept winning. They won four more American League pennants (1961, 1962, 1963, and 1964), and the World Series in 1961 and 1962.

When the great teams are discussed, the 1961 Yankees (**13C**) are always included. They won 109 games and rolled past the Cincinnati Reds in the World Series in five games. Their 240 home runs were a Major League record; and Whitey Ford had his best year with a 25-4 record, winning both the Cy Young and the World Series MVP awards. The most exciting part of the 1961 season, however, was the chase by Mickey Mantle and Roger Maris—the M&M Boys—after Babe Ruth's record of 60 home runs in a season, set back in 1927 **(23C)**. They swapped the lead throughout the season until mid-September when a hip injury forced Mantle out of the lineup. Mantle ended the season with a career high 54 home runs and Maris went on to break Ruth's record, hitting his 61st homer on the last day of the season **(12C)**. For his achievement, Maris won his second consecutive MVP award, the Hickok Belt, and was named the Sporting News Player of the Year.

Down Years, 1965 to 1995 *(Photos 12B, 13B, and 14B)*. Over the next 30 years, the Yankees would win only four pennants (1976, 1977, 1978, and 1981), and two World Series (1977 and 1978). These were difficult years. Thurman Munson **(14C)** and Jim "Catfish" Hunter **(13B)** were the most important players on these successful teams in the later years of the 1970s.

Munson **(14C)** was the "heart and soul" of the Yankees from 1969 until his tragic death in an airplane crash in 1979. Recognized for his gritty play, he was the American League's Rookie of the Year in 1969 and a seven-time All-Star. A superb defensive catcher, Munson won three Gold Gloves, and in 1971 had only a single error and nine passed balls. In 1976, he was named the Yankee Captain and was the American League's MVP. In his three World Series appearances, Munson batted .373, and his lifetime batting average was .292.

Jim "Catfish" Hunter **(13B)** came to the Yankees in 1975 by way of free agency from the Oakland Athletics where he had been a star pitcher on their World Series championship teams in 1972, 1973, and 1974. He was the first pitcher since Walter Johnson in 1915 to win 200 games before age 31. Between 1971 and 1975, Hunter had five consecutive 20 win seasons. In 1974, he was 25-12 with a 2.49 ERA, and won the Cy Young Award. His addition to the Yankee pitching staff in 1975 was fundamental to propelling them to the World Series in 1976, 1977, and 1978, and back-to-back World Series victories in 1977 and 1978. In all, Hunter played on five World Series championship teams with Oakland and the Yankees.

Don Mattingly **(12B)** was a great first baseman destined to unfortunately play on mediocre Yankee teams between 1982 and 1995. During his time with the Yankees they made the playoffs only once (1995). His inspired play—known as Donnie Ball—was the lone highlight for the fans to cheer. He was the Yankee Captain from 1991 until his retirement in 1995. In his 14 years in pinstripes, Mattingly hit .307, won nine Gold Gloves, three Silver Slugger awards, the 1984 batting title, and the 1985 MVP.

Joe Torre Years, 1996-2007 *(Photos 12A, 14A, and 14B)*. Joe Torre **(14A)** was the fourth great Yankee manager following in the tradition of Miller Huggins, Joe McCarthy, and Casey Stengel. After winning only four pennants and two World Series in the prior 30 years (1965-1995), Torre made the Yankees consistent champions again. During his reign—1996 through 2007—they won a total of 1,173 games and lost only 767 for a .605 winning percentage. They made the playoffs every year and won six pennants and four World Series, including three in a row (1998, 1999, and 2000). His 1998 team won 114 games and lost only 48 for a .704 win percentage.

Derek Jeter **(14B)** was the Yankee's all-time greatest shortstop. He was Rookie of the Year in 1996 and became the leader and face of the Yankees—if not all baseball—for the next two decades. Known as "The Captain", Jeter played on five World Series champions and had 3,465 career hits for a .310 lifetime batting average. He won five Gold Gloves and five Silver Slugger awards, among many other honors. In 2020, Jeter was elected to the Baseball Hall of Fame with the second highest vote total ever received—99.75 percent.

Mariano Rivera **(12A)** pitched for the Yankees from 1995 through 2013 and was the last player to wear No. 42. He was the best closer in the history of the game with 652 saves and his 2.21 career ERA is the lowest in the Modern Era. And he did it with one spectacularly effective pitch—a cut fastball delivered in the mid-90s, with pinpoint control. Rivera was elected to the Baseball Hall of Fame in 2019 by the only UNANIMOUS vote ever recorded.

Wall 3

Babe Ruth

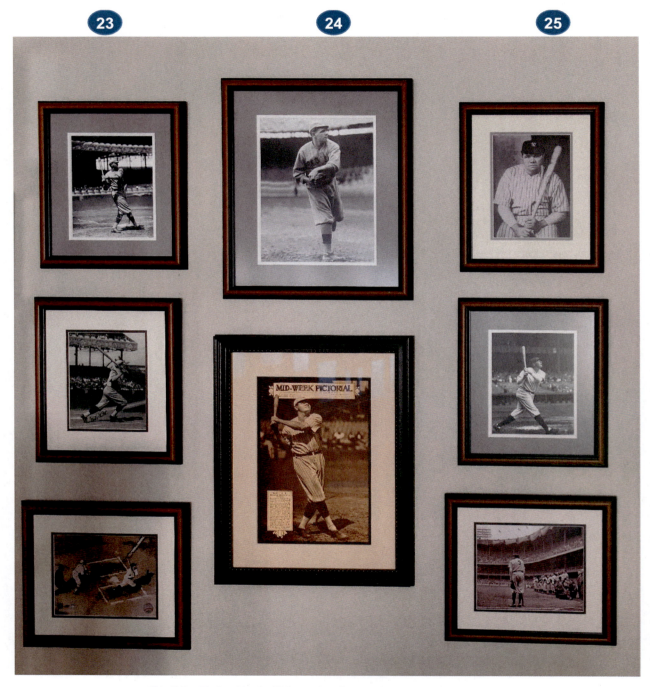

Wall 3: Babe Ruth *(Photo by Sean Kelley Photography)*.

Wall 3: Babe Ruth *(Columns 23-25)*. The photos of George Herman "Babe" Ruth, shown on the opposing page, date from his years with the Boston Red Sox through his tenure with the Yankees, and his final appearance at Yankee Stadium on Babe Ruth Day in 1948.

Ruth's time with the Boston Red Sox (1915-1919) is represented in the 1918 Charles M. Conlon photo **(23A)** of him swinging, and in the 1916 large frame shot **(24A)** of him pitching. While he was with the Red Sox, he was the best left-handed pitcher in the American League. His lifetime record was 94-36 with a 2.28 ERA. In 1916, he was 23-12 with a 1.75 ERA in 323 innings pitched. That season, Ruth also pitched nine shutouts—a record that lasted until 1978—longer than either his single season record of 60 home runs or his career total of 714. In 1917, he was just as good, winning 24 while losing only 13 with a 2.01 ERA in 326 innings. The Babe pitched on three Red Sox World championship teams: 1915, 1916, and 1918. Across the 1916 and 1917 World Series he pitched 29 and 2/3 consecutive scoreless innings, which was another long-standing record, not exceeded until 1961 by Whitey Ford. In 1918, while still primarily used as a pitcher, Ruth led the American League with 11 home runs. The value of his hitting though could not be denied, and the Red Sox made him a full-time outfielder in 1919 so he could play every day. Ruth responded by hitting 29 home runs—an unbelievable number in that era—while also leading the league with 113 RBIs, and batting .322.

His sale to the New York Yankees is illustrated in the 1920 photo **(23B)** of a still trim Ruth in a Yankee uniform. Needing cash, the Red Sox owner, Harry Frazee, sold the 24-year-old Ruth to the Yankees for the princely sum of $100,000. In his first season in New York, Ruth topped all expectations: 54 HRs, 135 RBIs, and a .376 batting average. Such an awesome display was never imagined for the sport. A new era was born—the Live Ball Era.

The original 1921 cover of *Mid-Week Pictorial* **(24B)** calls attention to Ruth's record year—the greatest offensive performance in the history of baseball: 59 HRs, .378 batting average, 168 RBIs, 177 runs, and 145 BBs. His statistics dipped to 35 home runs and just a .315 batting average in 1922; but in 1923 Ruth returned to form and hit 41 home runs and batted a career high .393, followed in 1924 by 46 home runs and a .378 batting average.

Ruth's trademark uppercut swing is highlighted in another Conlon photo, this one is from 1925 **(25B)**. Note Ruth's elevated eyes as he follows the soaring flight of the ball. Unfortunately 1925 would turn out to be an off-year for Ruth and the Yankees. Heading north with the club from spring training, Ruth collapsed near Asheville, North Carolina and required intestinal surgery. Some news accounts reported him dead. He played only 98 games in 1925 and hit but 25 homers; but bounced back in 1926, and through 1932 he continued his prodigious play. A version of this photo was the model for the Babe Ruth commemorative postage stamp issued by the United States Postal Service on July 6, 1983.

Two photos are from 1927: the classic studio full face **(25A)** taken by Nickolas Murray for the National Portrait Gallery; and one of Ruth hitting his record 60th home run at Yankee Stadium on September 30, 1927 **(23C)** off Tom Zachary of the Washington Senators.

Babe Ruth's farewell at Yankee Stadium on June 13, 1948 is poignantly captured in the Pulitzer Prize winning photo by Nathaniel Fein **(25C)**. The day celebrated the 25th anniversary of the opening of Yankee Stadium (1923)—The House That Ruth Built—and was the occasion to retire his No. 3. Dying from throat cancer, the hero stood, using a bat for a cane, and spoke just a few hoarse words. The moment was immortalized by Fein in this photograph, which he took from behind at a low angle from the dugout steps to prominently show Ruth's number, as the once mighty Babe bid farewell to a hushed crowd of 49,641 fans. Fein's shot has been called the most famous photograph in all sports. Ruth died two months later. His body lay in state for two days at the entrance of Yankee Stadium where an estimated 75,000 to 100,000 fans paid their respects.

Wall 4

Baseball in America

Wall 4: Baseball in America *(Photo by Sean Kelley Photography)*.

Wall 4: Baseball in America *(Columns 26-28)* is comprised of seven items from the late 19th and 20th centuries: three photos, two magazine covers, and two prints from popular periodicals.

The grand opening of Yankee Stadium **(26A)** was on April 18, 1923. From their initial founding as the New York Highlanders in 1903 through the 1912 season, the team played at Hilltop Park, located in Washington Heights between West 165th and 168th streets. When the New York Giants opened their renovated Polo Grounds in 1913, after the devastating fire of 1911, the Highlanders, now called the New York Yankees, agreed to a 10-year sublease. The arrangement worked so long as John McGraw was confident that his Giants would remain the city's favorite team. With Babe Ruth's arrival in New York in 1920, that changed drastically. The Yankees not only became American League champions in 1921, 1922, and 1923; they set new attendance records as well. In 1920, they were the first team to draw more than a million fans in a season (1,289,422), outdistancing the Giants, who then refused to renew their lease. Consequently, the Yankees began constructing their own ball park in May 1922, at East 161st St. and River Ave. in the Bronx. It was ready in just 11 months for a cost of $2,500,000. The announced crowd on Opening Day (April 18, 1923) was 74,200, with perhaps as many as 25,000 fans turned away. This was the largest crowd to ever attend a sporting event. New York no longer solely belonged to the New York Giants; and that fall, the Yankees defeated McGraw's Giants to win their first of 27 World Series.

President Franklin D. Roosevelt threw out the ceremonial first pitch at Griffith Stadium in Washington D.C., on April 19, 1938 **(26B)**. The tradition had started in 1910 with President William Howard Taft. President Roosevelt made a record eight opening day appearances. FDR was a lifelong baseball enthusiast as evidenced by the numerous baseball references found throughout his speeches. On January 14, 1942, soon after the attack on Pearl Harbor, Baseball Commissioner Kenesaw Mountain Landis asked Roosevelt if the National Pastime should be suspended, and the President immediately came to baseball's defense, replying: "I honestly feel that it would be best for the country to keep baseball going." Baseball was indeed played throughout the entire war, though the quality of play was appreciably diluted by the significant number of players in military service.

With the advent of radio, and later television, fans were brought closer to the game and play-by-play announcers became their intimate intermediaries. Two pioneers of the broadcast booth, Mel Allen in the foreground and Red Barber in the background **(26C)**, are caught in action doing a 1948 game between the Yankees and the Cleveland Indians. In 1978, Allen and Barber were the first recipients of baseball's highest honor for broadcasters—the Ford Frick Award from the Baseball Hall of Fame. Both were outstanding play-by-play men with distinctive styles and phrasing. Barber's approach was more reportorial and neutral; while Allen rooted for the home team and freely entered into the drama of the game. They called Yankee games together from 1954 to 1964.

Original prints and covers from *Harper's Weekly* and *Frank Leslie's Illustrated Newspaper* for 1885, 1886, and 1888 are in **(Columns 27 and 28)**. The depth of coverage devoted to baseball in these popular, high circulation, publications testifies to the general popularity of baseball in the United States before the end of the 19th century.

(27A, 28A, and 28B) are from the periodical *Harper's Weekly*, a self-styled "Journal of Civilization." A baseball scene of a batter, catcher, and umpire **(27A)** is featured on the cover of the July 1888 issue with the caption: "A Ball or Strike—Which?" A New York Giant sliding home against the Chicago White Sox **(28A)** is from the August 22, 1885 issue. And in **(28B)**, the great New York Giants' battery of the 1880s—Timothy J. Keefe and Buck Ewing—is set side by side in the October 20, 1888 issue.

(27B) is a cover of *Frank Leslie's Illustrated Newspaper*, May 8, 1886 (Caption: New York—Opening of the National League Baseball Season at the Polo Grounds, April, New York vs. Boston, Victorious Batsmen Carried on the Shoulders of their Admirers).

Part 2

Reference Indexes

1. Directory by Column and Row
2. Alphabetical List of Subjects

Reference Indexes

Introduction. The following Directory lists the 100 photographs sequentially by **Column (1-28)** and **Row (A-E)**. For each entry, the name of the player, team, or event, as well as the source of the photograph, if known, is provided.

Refer back to the orientation photos in Part 1: "Reading the Wall" to locate the photos on the walls; and ahead to Part 3: "Photo Gallery" for full-page reproductions of each photograph for closer study.

A number of the Directory entries are followed by references to the *Golden Age* and *Big Show*. They are abbreviated titles for collections of Charles M. Conlon photographs put together by Neal and Constance McCabe. Sixteen of the photos used in this project were taken by Conlon and these two books present information on him and his included photos. The full citations are: Neal McCabe and Constance McCabe, *Baseball's Golden Age: The Photographs of Charles M. Conlon* (New York: Harry N. Abrams, Inc., 1997); and Neal McCabe and Constance McCabe, *The Big Show: Charles M. Conlon's Golden Age Baseball Photographs* (New York: Abrams, 2011). The designation HoF refers to the Baseball Hall of Fame at Cooperstown, New York, the source for many of the photographs.

Wall 1: Baseball from 1903 to the mid-1970s. Above the couch are players and teams from both the American and National leagues, circa 1903 through the mid-1970s. There are 41 photos, moving chronologically oldest to more recent, from L to R, **Columns 1-11**.

1A. Three New York Giants (L to R: Christy Mathewson, John McGraw, and Joe "Iron Man" McGinnity; photo circa 1903)
1B. Honus Wagner facing right with bat in his hands (Photo 1 of 3, circa 1909)
1C. Eddie Collins
1D. Ty Cobb (1905 rookie season, photo by Daniel Hagerman)

2A. 1906 Chicago Cubs
2B. Honus Wagner full face (Photo 2 of 3, Bettmann photo)
2C. Napoleon "Larry" or "Nap" Lajoie (Photo by J. Taylor Green)
2D. "Shoeless" Joe Jackson in Cleveland uniform holding bat on shoulder (1913 photo by Charles M. Conlon, hand developed from glass plate by Celestial Images, see *Golden Age*, p. 154)

3A. Edward "Ted" Morgan Lewis (HoF photo)
3B. Honus Wagner swinging follow through (Photo 3 of 3)
3C. "Gorgeous" George Sisler (Cover of *Time Magazine*, March 30, 1925)
3D. Immortals at 1939 Hall of Fame ceremony at Cooperstown, New York (Seated, L to R: Eddie Collins, Babe Ruth, Connie Mack, and Cy Young; standing, L to R: Honus Wagner, Grover Cleveland Alexander, Tris Speaker, Nap Lajoie, George Sisler, and Walter Johnson; Ty Cobb was late and missed photo)

4A. Frank "Home Run" Baker (1910 photo by Charles M. Conlon, see *Golden Age*, p.80)
4B. Tris "The Gray Eagle" Speaker
4C. Rogers "The Raja" Hornsby (HoF photo)

5A. Connie Mack (HoF photo)
5B. Jimmie "Double X" Foxx (Photo 1 of 2)
5C. Charles "Chief" Bender (HoF photo)
5D. Walter "The Big Train" Johnson (Photo by Charles M. Conlon in 1910s, first generation photo from the original negative, The Conlon Portfolios)

6A. 1929 Philadelphia Athletics
6B. Three Philadelphia Athletics (L to R: Jimmie Foxx, Mickey Cochrane, and Al Simmons; HoF photo)
6C. Christy Mathewson (1911 photo by Charles M. Conlon, HoF photo, see *Golden Age*, p. 189)

7A. Robert Moses "Lefty" Grove (HoF photo)
7B. Jimmie Foxx (Photo 2 of 2)
7C. Grover Cleveland "Old Pete" Alexander
7D. Mordecai "Three Finger" Brown (HoF photo)

8A. Bill Terry (Press photo, September 27, 1936)
8B. Dizzy Dean (1932 photo by Charles M. Conlon, see *Golden Age*, p. 88)
8C. American League sluggers struck out in succession by Carl Hubbell at the 1934 All-Star

game (L to R: Al Simmons, Lou Gehrig, Babe Ruth, and Jimmie Foxx; a fifth strikeout victim, Joe Cronin, is not in the photo)
8D. Stan "The Man" Musial (Painting by John Falter in 1954, original is in the Baseball Hall of Fame, Cooperstown, NY; done as a cover for the *Saturday Evening Post*)

9A. Mel Ott (Photo rookie season by Charles M. Conlon)
9B. Carl "The Meal Ticket" Hubbell (1929 rookie photo by Charles M. Conlon, see *Golden Age*, p. 97)
9C. Hank Greenberg (Photo by Charles M. Conlon)
9D. Ted Williams (1939 rookie season by Charles M. Conlon, HoF photo, see *Golden Age*, p. 38)

10A. Leroy "Satchel" Paige
10B. Jackie Robinson stealing home (Game 1 of the 1955 World Series against the New York Yankees, Yogi Berra is the catcher, photo from Hulton Archive)
10C. Faye Dancer (Original photo signed and inscribed to Josie)
10D. Willie Mays sliding home (Bettmann photo)

11A. Joshua "Josh" Gibson
11B. Branch Rickey (HoF photo)
11C. Henry "Hank" Aaron

Wall 2: The New York Yankees from the 1920s to 2007. Above the TV, directly across from the couch. Moving L to R, in **Columns 12-22**, there are 44 photos dating from 2007 back to the 1920s.

12A. Mariano "Sand Man" Rivera (Original photo by Anthony J. Causi, signed by Rivera with certificate of authenticity)
12B. Don Mattingly
12C. Roger Maris hitting his 61st home run (October 1, 1961 at Yankee Stadium)

13B. Jim "Catfish" Hunter (Signed with certificate of authenticity)
13C. 1961 New York Yankees

14A. Joe Torre (Photo by Jed Jacobsohn)
14B. Derek Jeter (Photo by Ronald C. Modra)
14C. Thurman Munson tagging out Rico Petrocelli of the Boston Red Sox at Yankee Stadium
14D. Elston Howard and Whitey Ford (Original News Service photo, June 4, 1964)

15A. Mickey Mantle (Bettmann photo)
15B. Whitey Ford (Photo by Robert Riger)
15C. Three great managers (L to R: Joe McCarthy, Casey Stengel, and Bill Terry; HoF photo)
15D1. Yogi Berra (Press photo, December 5, 1955)
15D2. Vic "The Springfield Rifle" Raschi
15E1. Tommy "Old Reliable" Henrich
15E2. Charlie Keller (Press photo, September 17, 1943)

16A. Three Italians in the Yankee lineup (1936 photo, L to R: Joe DiMaggio, Frank Crosetti, and Tony Lazzeri; HoF photo)
16B. Red Rolfe (Press photo from 1937 World Series)
16C. Joe "Flash" Gordon making double play pivot at second base against the Chicago White Sox (Press photo July 29, 1946)
16D. Phil "Scooter" Rizzuto bunting (Signed with certificate of authenticity)
16E. Allie "Superchief" Reynolds (Signed with certificate of authenticity)

17A. Four Yankee Sluggers (L to R: Bill Dickey, Joe DiMaggio, Charlie Keller, and George Selkirk, photo taken September 21, 1939, Bettmann photo)
17B. Yankee infield 1930s (L to R: Red Rolfe, Tony Lazzeri, Frank Crosetti, and Lou Gehrig)
17C. Joe DiMaggio (1937 photo by Charles M. Conlon, see *Big Show*, p. 111)

18A. 1939 New York Yankees
18B. Spud Chandler (1938 photo by Charles M. Conlon, see *Golden Age*, p. 30)
18C. Joe DiMaggio swinging (Photo 1 of 3, singles vs. Senators on June 29, 1941 and extends hitting streak to 42 consecutive games; HoF photo)

19A. Vernon "Lefty" Gomez (Cover of *Time Magazine*, July 9, 1934)

19B. Three Yankees early 1930s (L to R: Bill Dickey, Lefty Gomez, and Lou Gehrig; HoF photo)
19C. Joe DiMaggio rounding first base (Photo 2 of 3, HoF photo)

20A. Joe McCarthy (HoF photo)
20B. Charles "Red" Ruffing (Signed with certificate of authenticity)
20C. Joe DiMaggio sliding home safely (Photo 3 of 3, June 16, 1941; HoF photo)

21A. Miller Huggins in street clothes facing right (HoF photo)
21B. Bob Meusel (Signed with certificate of authenticity)
21C. 1927 Yankee infield (L to R: Lou Gehrig, Tony Lazzeri, Mark Koenig, and Joe Dugan)
21D. Waite Hoyt (World Series 1926, signed with certificate of authenticity)
21E. Tony Lazzeri (HoF photo)

22A. 1927 New York Yankees
22B1. Lou Gehrig swinging (1934 photo by Charles M. Conlon, first generation photo from original negative, The Conlon Portfolios Conlon, see *Golden Age*, p. 178)
22B2. Lou Gehrig facing left (1925 photo by Charles M. Conlon, first generation photo from original negative, see *Golden Age*, p. 64)
22C. Yankee sluggers 1920s (L to R: Earle Combs, Bob Meusel, Lou Gehrig, and Babe Ruth; Bettmann photo)
22D. Herb Pennock (Official 1928 Yankee photo by Thorne, stamped *Sporting News*)
22E. Bill Dickey (1928 rookie year by Charles M. Conlon, see *Golden Age*, p. 193)

Wall 3: Babe Ruth. Facing left of the door to patio there are eight photos of Babe Ruth, **Columns 23-25**.

23A. Babe Ruth swinging for the Boston Red Sox (1918 Charles M. Conlon photo, first generation photo from original negative, The Conlon Portfolios, see *Baseball's Golden Age*, p. 52)
23B. Babe Ruth swinging for the New York Yankees in 1920 (HoF photo)

23C. Babe Ruth hitting 60th home run at Yankee Stadium, September 30, 1927

24A. Babe Ruth pitching for the Boston Red Sox in 1916
24B. Babe Ruth swinging in 1921 (Cover of *Mid-Week Pictorial: An Illustrated Weekly Published by The New York Times,* September 22, 1921)

25A. Babe Ruth full face (1927 studio photo by Nickolas Murray)
25B. Babe Ruth swinging for the New York Yankees (1925 photo by Charles M. Conlon, first generation photo from the original negative, The Conlon Portfolios, see *Big Show*, p. 33)
25C. Babe Ruth Day at Yankee Stadium, June 13, 1948 (Photo by Nathaniel Fein of the *New York Herald Tribune*, photo won the 1949 Pulitzer Prize)

Wall 4: Baseball in America. Facing right of the patio door, in **Columns 26-28**, there are seven images.

26A. Opening day of the new Yankee Stadium, April 18, 1923
26B. President Franklin Roosevelt prepares to throw out opening-day ball on April 19, 1938 (Griffith Stadium in Washington DC, Senators hosted the Philadelphia Athletics, Bettmann photo)
26C. Mel Allen foreground and Red Barber background calling a game between the New York Yankees and the Cleveland Indians in 1948 at Cleveland Stadium (HoF photo)

27A. Original cover of the magazine *Harper's Weekly*, July 28, 1888 (Caption: A Ball or a Strike—Which?)
27B. Original cover of *Frank Leslie's Illustrated Newspaper*, May 8, 1886 (Caption: New York—Opening of the National League Baseball Season at the Polo Grounds, April, New York vs. Boston, Victorious Batsmen Carried on the Shoulders of their Admirers)

28A. Original woodcut from *Harper's Weekly*, August 22, 1885 (Caption: The Winning Run—'"How is It Umpire?")

28 B. Original woodcut from *Harper's Weekly*, October 20, 1888 (Caption: The Winning Battery of the New York Baseball Team, pitcher L is Timothy J. Keefe, catcher R is William Ewing)

Alphabetical List of Subjects

Aaron, Henry (11C)
Alexander, Grover Cleveland (3D, 7C)
Allen, Mel (26C)
Athletics, Philadelphia 1929 (6A)

Baker, Frank "Home Run" (4A)
Barber, Red (26C)
Bender, Charles "Chief" (5C)
Berra, Yogi (10B, 15D1)
Brown, Mordecai "Three Finger" (7D)

Chandler, Spud (18B)
Cobb, Ty (1D)
Cochrane, Mickey (6B)
Collins, Eddie (1C, 3D)
Combs, Earle (22C)
Crosetti, Frank (16A, 17B)
Cubs, Chicago 1906 (2A)

Dancer, Faye (10C)
Dean, Dizzy (8B)
Dickey, Bill (17A, 19B, 22E)
DiMaggio, Joe (16A, 17A, 17C, 18C, 19C, 20C)
Dugan, Joe (21C)

Ewing, William (28B)

Ford, Whitey (14D, 15B)
Foxx, Jimmie (5B, 6B, 7B, and 8C)

Gehrig, Lou (8C, 17B, 19B, 21C, 22B1, 22B2, 22C)
Gibson, Josh (11A)
Gomez, Vernon "Lefty" (19A, 19B)
Gordon, Joe "Flash" (16C)
Greenberg, Hank (9C)
Grove, Robert Moses "Lefty" (7A)

Henrich, Tommy (15E1)
Hornsby, Rogers (4C)
Howard, Elston (14D)
Hoyt, Waite (21D)
Hubbell, Carl (9B)
Huggins, Miller (21A)
Hunter, Jim "Catfish" (13B)

Jackson, Joseph Jefferson "Shoeless Joe" (2D)
Jeter, Derek (14B)
Johnson, Walter "The Big Train" (3D, 5D)

Keefe, Timothy J. (28B)
Keller, Charlie (15E2, 17A)
Koenig, Mark (21C)

Lajoie, Napoleon (2C, 3D)
Lazzeri, Tony (16A, 17B, 21C, 21E)
Lewis, Edward "Ted" Morgan (3A)

Mack, Connie (3D, 5A)
Mantle, Mickey (15A)
Maris, Roger (12C)
Mathewson, Christy (1A, 6C)
Mattingly, Don (12B)
Mays, Willie (10D)
McCarthy, Joe (15C, 20A)
McGinnity, Joe "Iron Man" (1A)
McGraw, John (1A)
Meusel, Bob "Long Bob" (21B, 22C)
Munson, Thurman (14C)
Musial, Stan "The Man" (8D)

Ott, Mel (9A)

Paige, Leroy "Satchel" (10A)
Pennock, Herb (22D)
Polo Grounds (27B)

Raschi, Vic "The Springfield Rifle" (15D2)
Reynolds, Allie "Superchief" (16E)
Rickey, Branch (11B)
Rizzuto, Phil "The Scooter" (16D)
Rolfe, Red (16B, 17B)
Rivera, Mariano "The Sand Man" (12A)
Robinson, Jackie (10B)
Roosevelt, Franklin D. (26B)
Ruffing, Charles "Red" (20B)
Ruth, Babe (3D, 8C, 22C, 23A, 23B, 23C, 24A, 24B, 25A, 25B, 25C)

Selkirk, George (17A)
Simmons, Al (6B, 8C)
Sisler, "Gorgeous" George (3C, 3D)
Speaker, Tris (3D, 4B)
Stengel, Casey "The Old Professor" (15C)

Terry, Bill (8A, 15C)
Torre, Joe (14A)

Wagner, Honus (1B, 2B, 3B, 3D)
Williams, Ted (9D)

Yankees, New York 1961 (13C)
Yankees, New York 1939 (18A)
Yankees, New York 1927 (22A)
Yankee Stadium April 18, 1923 (26A)
Young, Cy (3D)

Part 3

Photo Gallery

Three New York Giants, 1A

(L to R: Christy Mathewson, John McGraw, and Joe "Iron Man" McGinnity; Photo circa 1903)

Honus Wagner facing right with bat in his hands, 1B

(Photo 1 of 3, circa 1909)

Eddie Collins, 1C

Ty Cobb, 1D

(1905 rookie season, photo by Daniel Hagerman)

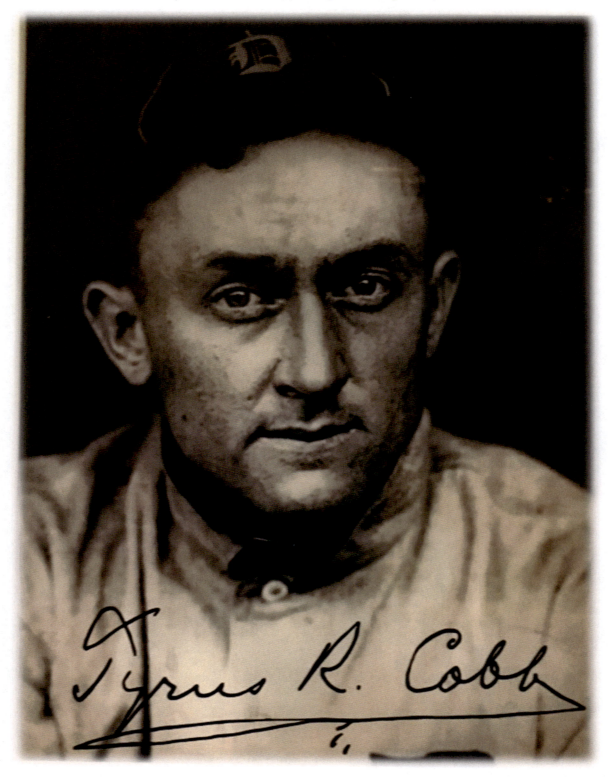

1906 Chicago Cubs, 2A

Honus Wagner full face, 2B

(Photo 2 of 3, Bettmann photo)

Napoleon "Nap" Lajoie, 2C

(Photo by J. Taylor Green)

"Shoeless" Joe Jackson in Cleveland uniform holding bat on shoulder, 2D

(1913 photo by Charles M. Conlon, hand developed from glass plate by Celestial Images, see *Golden Age*, p. 154)

Edward "Ted" Morgan Lewis, 3A

(HoF photo)

Honus Wagner swinging follow through, 3B

(Photo 3 of 3)

"Gorgeous" George Sisler, 3C

(Cover of *Time Magazine*, March 30, 1925)

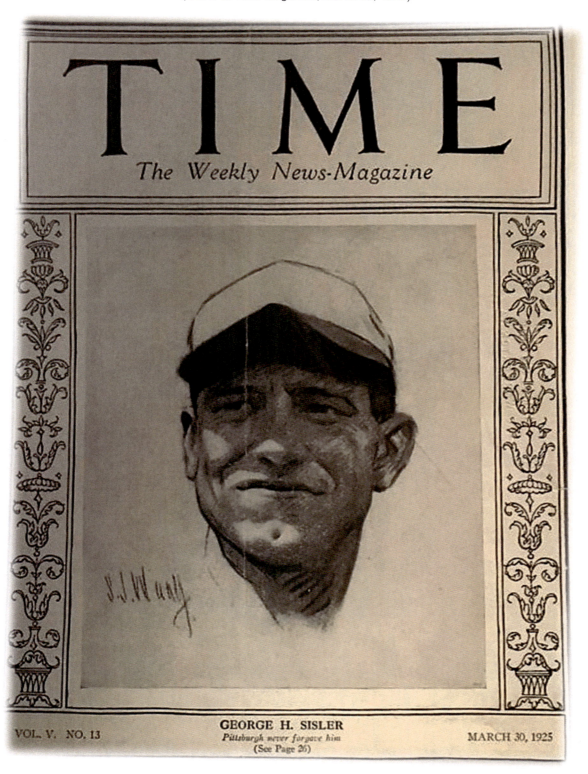

Immortals at 1939 Hall of Fame ceremony at Cooperstown, NY, 3D

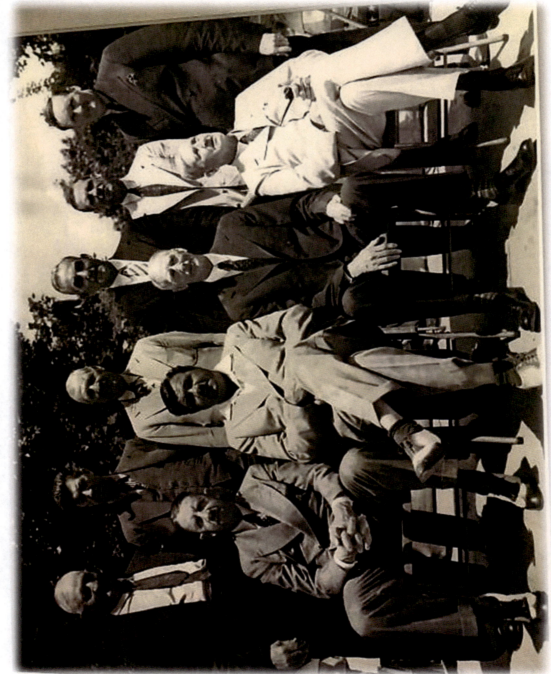

(Seated, L to R: Eddie Collins, Babe Ruth, Connie Mack, and Cy Young; standing: L to R, Honus Wagner, Grover Cleveland Alexander, Tris Speaker, Nap Lajoie, George Sisler, and Walter Johnson; Ty Cobb was late and missed photo)

Frank "Home Run" Baker, 4A

(1910 photo by Charles M. Conlon, see *Golden Age*, p.80)

Tris "The Gray Eagle" Speaker, 4B

Rogers "The Rajah" Hornsby, 4C

(HoF photo)

Connie Mack, 5A

(HoF photo)

Jimmie "Double X" Foxx, 5B

Charles "Chief" Bender, 5C

(HoF photo)

Walter "The Big Train" Johnson, 5D

(Photo by Charles M. Conlon in 1910s, first generation photo
from the original negative, The Conlon Portfolios)

1929 Philadelphia Athletics, 6A

Three Philadelphia Athletics, 6B
(L to R: Jimmie Foxx, Mickey Cochrane, and Al Simmons; HoF photo)

Christy Mathewson, 6C

(1911 photo by Charles M. Conlon, HoF photo, see *Golden Age*, p. 189)

Robert Moses "Lefty" Grove, 7A
(HoF photo)

Jimmie Foxx, 7B

Grover Cleveland "Old Pete" Alexander, 7C

Mordecai "Three Finger" Brown, 7D

(HoF photo)

Bill Terry, 8A

(Press photo, September 27, 1936)

Dizzy Dean, 8B

(1932 photo by Charles M. Conlon, see *Golden Age*, p. 88)

American League sluggers struck out in succession by Carl Hubbell at the 1934 All-Star game, 8C

(L to R: Al Simmons, Lou Gehrig, Babe Ruth, and Jimmie Foxx; a fifth strikeout victim, Joe Cronin, is not in the photo)

Stan "The Man" Musial, 8D

(Painting by John Falter in 1954, original is in the Baseball Hall of Fame, Cooperstown, NY; done as a cover for the *Saturday Evening Post*)

Mel Ott, 9A

(Photo rookie season by Charles M. Conlon)

Carl "The Meal Ticket" Hubbell, 9B
(1929 rookie photo by Charles M. Conlon, see *Golden Age*, p. 97)

Hank Greenberg, 9C

(Photo by Charles M. Conlon)

Ted Williams, 9D

(1939 rookie season by Charles M. Conlon, HoF photo, see *Golden Age*, p. 38)

Leroy "Satchel" Paige, 10A

Jackie Robinson stealing home, 10B

(Game 1 of the 1955 World Series against the New York Yankees, Yogi Berra is the catcher, photo from Hulton Archive)

Faye Dancer, 10C

(Original photo signed and inscribed to Josie)

Willie Mays sliding home, 10D

(Bettmann photo)

Joshua "Josh" Gibson, 11A

Branch Rickey, 11B
(HoF photo)

Henry "Hank" Aaron, 11C

Mariano "Sand Man" Rivera, 12A

(Original photo by Anthony J. Causi, signed by Rivera with certificate of authenticity)

Don Mattingly, 12B

Roger Maris hitting his 61st homerun, 12C
(October 1, 1961 at Yankee Stadium)

Jim "Catfish" Hunter, 13B

(Signed with certificate of authenticity)

1961 New York Yankees, 13C

Joe Torre, 14A

(Photo by Jed Jacobsohn)

Derek Jeter, 14B
(Photo by Ronald C. Modra)

Thurman Munson tagging out Rico Petrocelli at Yankee Stadium, 14C

Elston Howard and Whitey Ford, 14D

(Original News Service photo, June 4, 1964)

Mickey Mantle, 15A
(Bettmann photo)

Whitey Ford, 15B
(Photo by Robert Riger)

Three Great Managers, 15C

(L to R: Joe McCarthy, Casey Stengel, and Bill Terry)

Yogi Berra, 15D1

(Press photo, December 5, 1955)

Vic "The Springfield Rifle" Raschi, 15D2

Tommy "Old Reliable" Henrich, 15E1

Charlie Keller, 15E2

(Press photo, September 17, 1943)

Three Italians in the Yankee lineup, 16A
(1936 photo, L to R: Joe DiMaggio, Frank Crosetti, and Tony Lazzeri; HoF photo)

Red Rolfe, 16B

(Press photo from 1937 World Series)

Joe "Flash" Gordon making double play pivot at second base against the Chicago White Sox, 16C

(Press photo July 29, 1946)

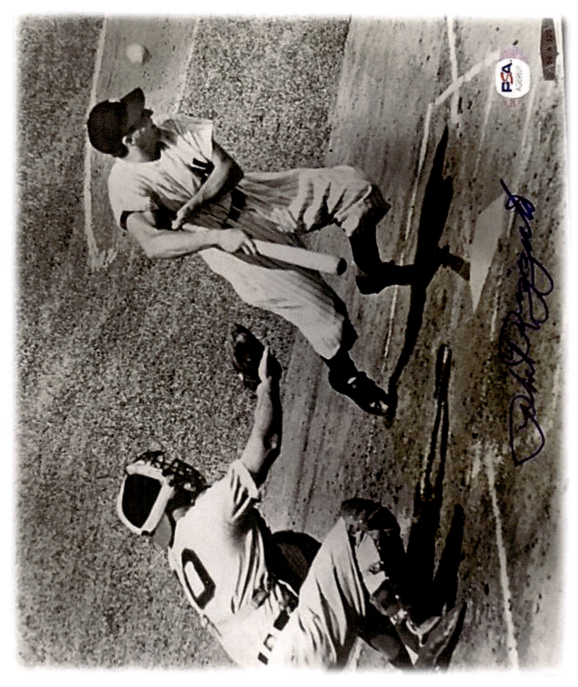

Phil " Scooter" Rizzuto bunting, 16D
(Signed with certificate of authenticity)

Allie "Superchief" Reynolds, 16E
(Signed with certificate of authenticity)

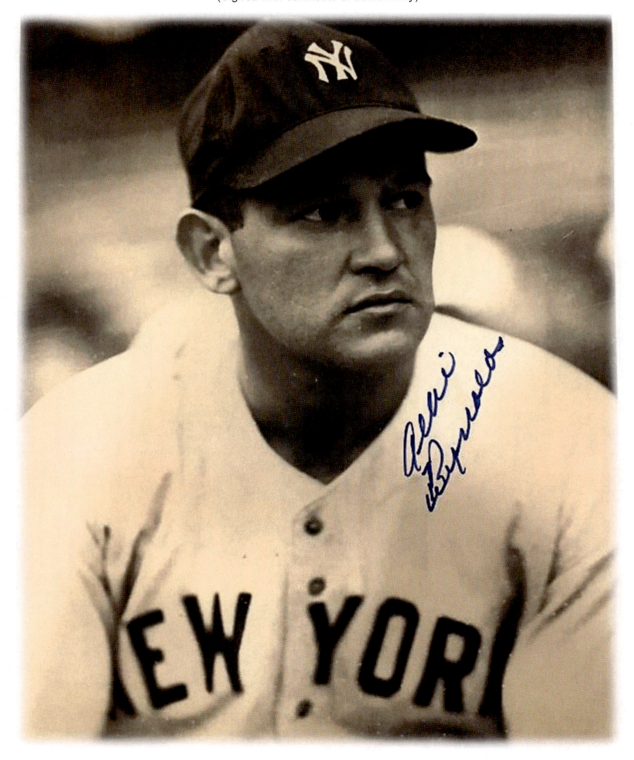

Four Yankee Sluggers, 17A

(L to R: Bill Dickey, Joe DiMaggio, Charlie Keller, and George Selkirk, photo taken September 21, 1939, Bettmann photo)

Yankee infield 1930s, 17B

(L to R: Red Rolfe, Tony Lazzeri, Frank Crosetti, and Lou Gehrig)

Joe DiMaggio, 17C

(1937 photo by Charles M. Conlon, see *Big Show*, p. 111)

1939 New York Yankees, 18A

Spud Chandler, 18B

(1938 photo by Charles M. Conlon, see *Golden Age*, p. 30)

Joe DiMaggio swinging, 18C

(Photo 1 of 3, singles vs. Senators on June 29, 1941 and extends hitting streak to 42 consecutive games; HoF photo)

Vernon "Lefty" Gomez, 19A

(Cover of *Time Magazine*, July 9, 1934)

Three Yankees early 1930s, 19B

(L to R: Bill Dickey, Lefty Gomez, and Lou Gehrig; HoF photo)

Joe DiMaggio rounding first base, 19C
(Photo 2 of 3, HoF photo)

Joe McCarthy, 20A
(HoF photo)

Charles "Red" Ruffing, 20B

(Signed with certificate of authenticity)

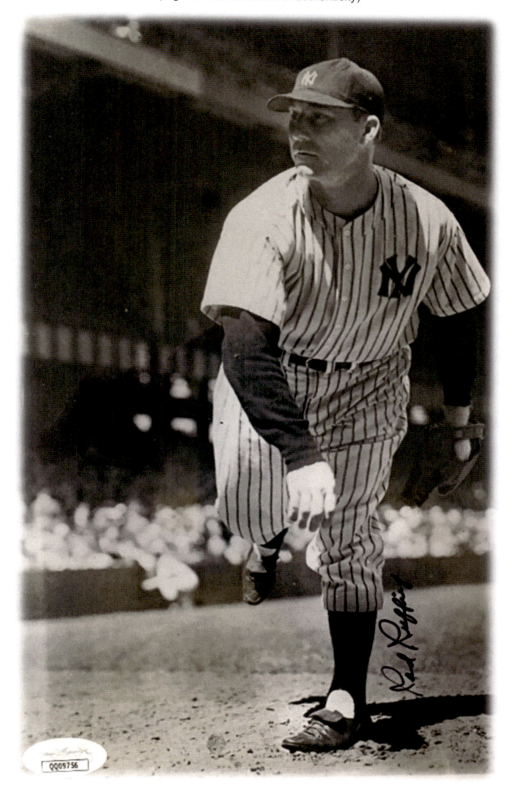

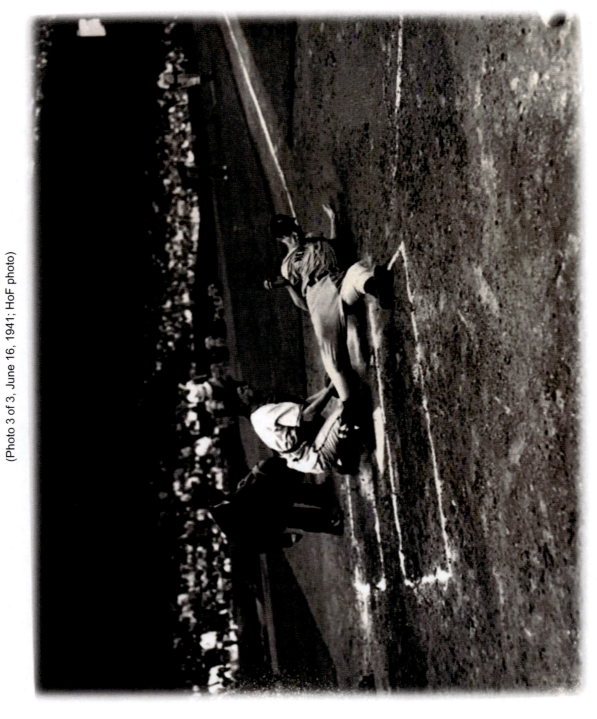

Joe DiMaggio sliding home safely, 20C

(Photo 3 of 3, June 16, 1941; HoF photo)

Miller Huggins in street clothes facing right, 21A

(HoF photo)

Bob Meusel, 21B
(Signed with certificate of authenticity)

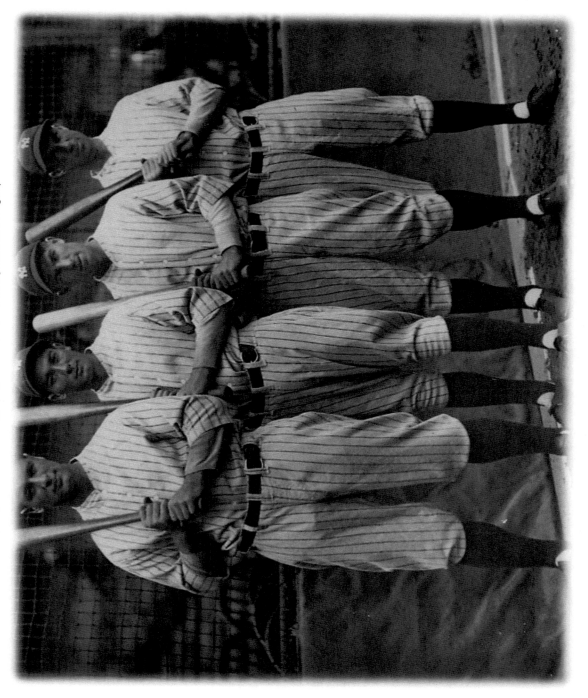

1927 Yankee infield, 21C

(L to R: Lou Gehrig, Tony Lazzeri, Mark Koenig, and Joe Dugan)

Waite Hoyt, 21D

(World Series 1926, signed with certificate of authenticity)

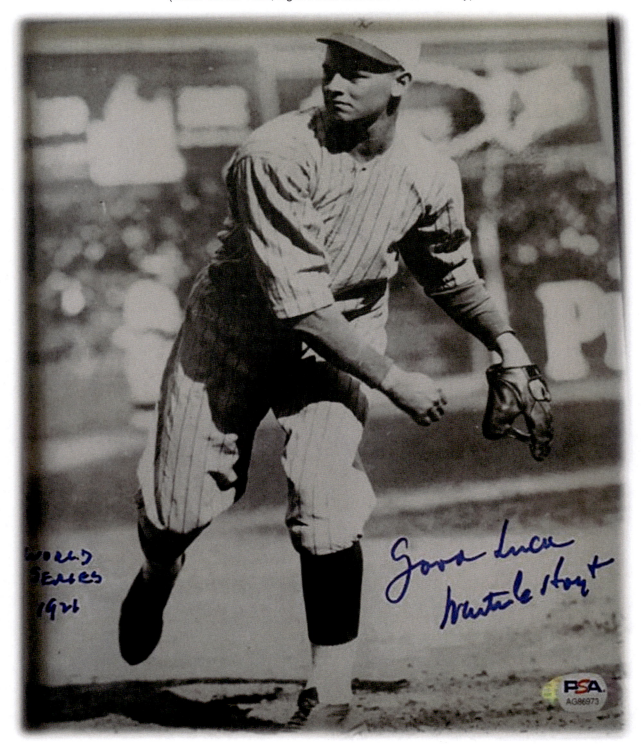

Tony Lazzeri, 21E

(HoF photo)

1927 New York Yankees, 22A

Lou Gehrig swinging, 22B1

(1934 photo by Charles M. Conlon, first generation photo from original negative,
The Conlon Portfolios, see *Golden Age*, p. 178)

Lou Gehrig facing left, 22B2

(1925 photo by Charles M. Conlon, first generation photo from original negative, see *Golden Age*, p. 64)

Yankee sluggers 1920s, 22C

(L to R: Earle Combs, Bob Meusel, Lou Gehrig, and Babe Ruth; Bettmann photo)

Herb Pennock, 22D

(Official 1928 Yankee photo by Thorne, stamped *Sporting News*)

Bill Dickey, 22E

(1928 rookie year by Charles M. Conlon, see *Golden Age*, p. 193)

Babe Ruth swinging for the Boston Red Sox, 23A

(1918 Charles M. Conlon photo, first generation photo from original negative,
The Conlon Portfolios, see *Baseball's Golden Age*, p. 52)

Babe Ruth swinging for the New York Yankees in 1920, 23B
(HoF photo)

Picturing Baseball: A Personal View in 100 Photographs

Babe Ruth hitting 60th home run at Yankee Stadium, September 30, 1927, 23C

Babe Ruth pitching for the Boston Red Sox in 1916, 24A

(Record of 23 and 12 with 1.75 ERA in 323 innings pitched that year)

Babe Ruth swinging in 1921, 24B

(Cover of *Mid-Week Pictorial: An Illustrated Weekly Published by The New York Times*, September 22, 1921)

Babe Ruth full face, 25A
(1927 photo by Nickolas Murray)

Babe Ruth swinging for the New York Yankees, 25B

(1925 photo by Charles M. Conlon, first generation photo from original negative,
The Conlon Portfolios, see *Big Show*, p. 33)

Babe Ruth Day at Yankee Stadium, June 13, 1948, 25C

(Photo by Nathaniel Fein of the *New York Herald Tribune*, photo won the 1949 Pulitzer Prize)

Opening day of the new Yankee Stadium, April 18, 1923, 26A

President Franklin D. Roosevelt prepares to throw out opening-day ball on April 19, 1938, 26B

(Griffith Stadium in Washington DC, Senators hosted the Philadelphia Athletics, Bettmann photo)

Mel Allen foreground and Red Barber background calling a game between the New York Yankees and the Cleveland Indians in 1948 at Cleveland Stadium, 26C

(HoF photo)

Original cover of *Harper's Weekly*, July 28, 1888, 27A

(Caption: A Ball or a Strike—Which?)

Original cover of *Frank Leslie's Illustrated Newspaper*, May 8, 1886, 27B

(Caption: New York—Opening of the National League Baseball Season at the Polo Grounds, April, New York vs. Boston, Victorious Batsmen Carried on the Shoulders of their Admirers)

Original woodcut from *Harper's Weekly*, August 22, 1885, 28A

(Caption: The Winning Run—' " How is It Umpire?")

Original woodcut from *Harper's Weekly*, October 20, 1888, 28B

(Caption: The Winning Battery of the New York Baseball Team, pitcher L is Timothy J. Keefe, catcher R is William Ewing)

Made in the USA
Columbia, SC
25 August 2024

25ffcbe8-3717-462c-b8ef-153e3f031437R01